Perpetual Photographs

Nina Strand

Objektiv #21

1.
The inspirational photograph

Perpetual Photographs takes as its inspiration the column, 'Sinnbilde' (On my Mind), which we presented in the very first issues of Objektiv. Here, we invited different people on the art scene to write about an image that they couldn't stop thinking about. We reignited the column last year in Objektiv's 10th year, as the ocean of images continued to swell, and the contributions we received inspired me to look more closely at images, interviews, impressions that are still on my mind.

When I interviewed MoMA curator Sarah Meister about the 2012 edition of *New Photography,* she said something I've been thinking about ever since.[1] She called today's generation of photographers 'the real Pictures Generation', since they've grown up truly surrounded by images. She also said that since photography is both old and new at the same time, the history of photography can be written in many different ways.

This interview took place eight years ago. Since then, we've witnessed a change. Big institutions are offering space and resources to lesser-known artists of the previous generation, giving them the attention they should have received in their time. Marta Gili, at the time director of the Jeu de Paume, Paris, confirmed this development in an interview I did with her for the seventeenth issue of Objektiv, which investigated the practice of exhibiting camera-based art.[2] Gili had also made a goal of showing the work of men and women on an equal basis. She was certain that the effects of the #metoo movement would reach all art institutions. She predicted that in a few years' time, we'll see that many museums that have never thought about this issue before will begin to work on showing more women, adding that many of her colleagues are aware that they have to do this as a responsibility if they wish to remain in the mainstream.

Sarah Charlesworth
A step towards this change was the 2015 exhibition *Sarah Charlesworth: Doubleworld* at the New Museum in New York. Charlesworth (1947–2013) was at that time not well known in Europe. Walking through the rooms, I wondered how she could have gone so unnoticed, in spite of her large contribution to our photographic history, being a peer of the Pictures Generation artists but never as famous as Cindy Sherman or Richard Prince. I spent a long time in the room dedicated to her *Stills* series from 1980, rephotographed and vastly enlarged newspaper cuttings of people falling or jumping from buildings. I was

especially drawn to *Unidentified Woman, Hotel Corona de Aragon, Madrid, 1980*. A curator, Matthew Witkovsky, has described these images as cheating death, 'Frozen by a camera shutter, their [the victims'] images can offer hope. It stills the moment so the end never comes.'[3]

Charlesworth's work resonates with that of contemporary artists such as Roe Etheridge and Elad Lassry. The latter mentioned her influence when I interviewed him.[4] He called his photographs a way to comment on the world, which resonates with Charlesworth's approach. Her way of manipulating her photographs caused many to question their truth, but as she herself said: 'I don't think of myself as a photographer. I've engaged questions regarding photography's role in culture ... but it's an engagement with a problem rather than a medium.'[5]

Her show in New York was still fresh on my mind when I went to see her almost completely white images in the exhibition *Sarah Charlesworth Selected by Liz Deschenes* at Campoli Presti in Paris in November 2016. While she was alive, Charlesworth never exhibited her work in a solo format in Paris. I saw the show on a Friday afternoon a few weeks after Paris Photo, and it acted as a cleanse after the overwhelming sea of impressions that such a festival offers. In the press release Deschenes, who was a friend and colleague of Charlesworth at the School of Visual Arts for many years, wrote that Charlesworth's influential body of work deconstructed the conventions of photography and helped establish the medium's centrality.[6] Deschenes had selected works from Charlesworth's *0+1* series, explaining that their fragility responds to the uncertain economy of images, which can either accelerate their reproduction or make them disappear over time. Deschenes told me she purposely chose a series that does not reproduce well – it has to be seen in person. All the images point to beginnings and endings.[7] Charlesworth herself has said that the series explored ideas about the beginnings of an image, almost like image degree zero. From notes that she wrote about the project, we learn that the title *0+1* comes in part from Roland Barthes' book *Writing Degree Zero*:

> Zero is the uninscribed. Language, Barthes writes, starts with an undifferentiated field. Language, pictorial or cursive, begins with a moment of inscription, making a mark. These images are suggestive of primary human representations or conceptions. The images I have

Sarah Charlesworth, *Unidentified Woman, Hotel Corona de Aragón, Madrid*, 1980. Courtesy the Estate of Sarah Charlesworth and Campoli Presti, London/Paris.

Sarah Charlesworth, *Bough,* 2000.
Courtesy the Estate of Sarah Charlesworth and Campoli Presti, London/Paris.

chosen to use as primary orientations are because they appeal to me. They are choices. 0+1 also refers to millennial thoughts (ending/ beginning) of human ideas of self and world. They can be seen as memories or traces of 'past' icons or as prototypes, or as choices, affirmations for the future. They are very clearly trying to find a still moment, a quiet state of mind in the face of a society of information and image overload.[8]

The series *0+1* marks a point in Charlesworth's life and career when her approach to photography became more meditative.[9] She would often spend hours or days on a single shot, carefully constructing the still life, typically shooting several frames, processing her film, then rephotographing. She normally worked alone in the studio, with nothing to disrupt her process, Matthew C. Lange told me over a FaceTime in April this year. Charlesworth taught Lange at the School of Visual Arts, and he worked as her assistant for three years. He has been her estate manager for six years. He agrees that she never got the attention she deserved, adding that her iconography represents textured, layered meanings. Her photographs in *0+1* revisit many of the iconic images with which she worked in her *Objects of Desire* series throughout the 1980s, in which she isolated cut-out images on single-coloured backgrounds. This makes *0+1* a pivotal series, connecting her early work to her late-career work, he explains.

In *0+1,* the almost linguistic dimension of the photographs is important. Working in analogue just before the digital age, Charlesworth tried six or seven different types of film to get the right effect. Lange elaborates on how she photographed obsessively, getting the correct exposures and then printed every edition all at once. She often presented a challenge for herself, creating conditions in which it was difficult to photograph, and where a certain level of meditation and attention was required. Lange believes that she was learning how to ground herself through making the picture, and she continued to do this in all of her subsequent series. This is how she established the method that would guide her through the rest of her career. She made *0+1* on the edge of the millennium, and all the uncertainty that came with it. It still feels highly relevant, and was one of the important pieces for her. It was made with an idea of looking slowly. Lange tells me how pleased she would have been with the Paris show, and to be represented by Paula Cooper, a New York gallery with which she always hoped to show.

Carrie Mae Weems, *Untitled (Man and Mirror)*, from *Kitchen Table Series,* 1990.
Courtesy of the artist and Jack Shainman Gallery, New York.

Carrie Mae Weems

Another New York-based photographer from the Pictures generation is Carrie Mae Weems. She has not only inspired artists who use themselves in their work, but also contributed to the fight against racism. As the first African-American woman to have held a retrospective at the Guggenheim (2014), she uses multiple media (photography, video, digital imagery, text, fabric and more) to explore themes of cultural identity, sexism, class, political systems, family relationships and the consequences of power.[10]

During the COVID crisis she is working on a public art project titled RESIST COVID / TAKE 6! with new portraits printed on flyers, posters and billboards focusing on the impact of the virus on black communities. The title refers to the requirement to keep at least six feet apart from one another. In an interview with Harpers Bazaar, she explains that her campaign:

> really arose out of a conversation with a very close friend, Pierre Loving, about the impact of COVID-19 on people of colour and what we could do about it. COVID-19 is not an equal opportunity virus. The numbers are staggering. For example, there was a report from Chicago in early April that 72 percent of people killed in that city by the coronavirus were Black, despite making up less than a third of its population. I understood immediately that our mission was to create an artist-driven public awareness campaign that attempts to get information into the hands of the most impacted.[11]

When Nasher Art Museum at Duke University in North Carolina had to close due to the virus, it initiated its first outdoor exhibition instead, and also launched Weems' campaign through large-scale banners, window clings, posters, street signs and more. As Marshall N. Price, Nancy A. Nasher and David J. Haemisegger Curator of Modern and Contemporary Art enthusiastically write me: 'RESIST COVID / TAKE 6! is an effective way to reach our audiences safely outdoors, as our museum is closed at the moment. The project helps to combat misperceptions about the COVID-19 virus, celebrates front line workers, raises issues of public health and racial inequities, and underscores how art can function as a public awareness campaign.'[12]

RESIST COVID / TAKE 6! at the Nasher Museum of Art at Duke University.
Photo by J. Caldwell.

Dora Maar

When I interviewed Eleonor Coppola about her exhibition *Circle of Memory,* shown at Fotografiska, Stockholm, in the summer of 2011, she talked about her frustration at not getting enough time and space to make art due to the career of her husband, Francis Ford Coppola. At one point she even toyed with the idea of putting her children in a gallery with the sign: 'My most important work ever'.[13] Some years later, when I was living in Paris and reading and learning about several Parisian artist's wives who could have had brilliant careers had the time been different, these words resonated deeply. They also came to mind when I went to see the great retrospective of Dora Maar at Centre Pompidou in the late summer of 2019. Too often identified merely as Pablo Picasso's muse and partner, whose career was only fully understood after her death, with the sale of her archive and, more recently, with research into her paintings and works on paper. As her friend Paul Eluard wrote in a dedication to her, Maar 'holds every image in her hands'.[14]

Maar's photograph on the exhibition catalogue, *Untitled* (Fashion photograph), c. 1935, was of a woman dressed in an evening gown with a star as her head. I was curious about how she took a fashion photograph like this in Paris, in those times. I asked curator Emma Lewis from Tate Modern – where the show went after Paris – to tell me more about Maar. She explained that Maar's lifetime spanned almost the whole of the twentieth century and she found it fascinating to map her life and career onto the social, political, and technological developments over the decades: developments in camera and print technologies, women's changing roles in society, the political climate of 1930s and postwar France, the company that Maar was keeping, where her professional opportunities came from at different points of time, and the art and philosophy with which she was coming into contact.[15]

Maar exhibited her street and surrealist photographs regularly throughout the 1930s and was one of the few photographers to be included in the major international surrealist exhibitions throughout the 1930s. In fact, she was the only photographer to be included in all six. She then exhibited her painting and works on paper throughout the 1940s and 1950s in Paris, London and Amsterdam, which were well received by critics. The next time her work was exhibited was in a group show on the avant-garde in 1980, when the interest in her surrealist photography slowly began to pick up, with a substantial solo exhibition mounted in Valencia in 1995, curated by her biographer Victoria Combalía.

DORA
MAAR

EDITED BY DAMARICE AMAO,
AMANDA MADDOX, AND
KAROLINA ZIEBINSKA-LEWANDOWSKA

Dora Maar exhibition catalogue, by Damarice Amao, Amanda Maddox,
Karolina Ziebinska-Lewandowska.

The lack of recognition, Lewis tells me, was in part due to the fact that Maar made the conscious decision, in her later years, not to conduct interviews (in part because she was bored by being asked about Picasso); she also declined some exhibitions. Her biography was complicated by myth and anecdote, and important aspects of her practice were overlooked or ignored. Lewis was heartened to find out, though, that she did have faith that her work would be recognised in time.

She hopes that the current tendency of institutions to give major retrospectives to women and artists of colour is not a 'trend', but an approach that will be sustained. When I interviewed Lewis in 2017 she was determined that more women and also, lesser-known figures should be represented at Tate, and showing Maar must make a good step towards this.[16] When Tate Modern opened in 2000, a 'timeline of art history' was prominently displayed in one of the concourse areas. As Tate Modern celebrates its twentieth anniversary, its approach has completely changed: curators now think in terms of histories, plural.

Rediscovery is an interesting concept, too, in terms of historiography for Lewis. Conversations about reviving forgotten histories sometimes overlook the fact that a previous generation of curators and scholars may have worked hard to unearth particular stories, but then they are forgotten again. Every generation of curators is working in a different context, attending to different questions of the time, and in Lewis' opinion a part of their responsibility as curators and historians is to connect their work with the research and scholarship that has come before.[17]

In the January issue of Frieze, deputy editor Amy Sherlock writes that amongst the more positive changes she has seen during the past decade is our rediscovery of female artists and the fact that the market had finally woken up to black creativity.[18] Jennifer Higgie, Frieze's editor at large has researched female artists for years. She runs the magazine's podcast, *Bow Down: Women in Art History* about significant women artists from the past who deserve attention. Women have been expressing themselves since the beginning of time, the podcast's introduction goes, yet most people struggle to name even one non-male artist from before the twentieth century. The podcast is developed from Higgie's Instagram account honouring female artists. She tells me that six years ago she set herself the task of

Dora Maar at Tate Modern installation view, 2019. Photo: Tate Photography.

finding the birthday of a woman artist every day. It was a challenge that was both illuminating and frustrating, since most of them have effectively been written out of art history. Asking her podcast guests – artists, art historians, filmmakers and writers – to nominate a female artist from the past to whom we should all 'bow down' has been a pleasure and an education. She is still learning so much about these extraordinary artists, who often had to battle hard to make a living and gain recognition. There is still a lot of work to be done in recognising artists who have been ignored by the canon – not only women, but also people of colour and those who have worked outside Western mainstreams. I bow down to Higgie for keeping this research going – and also to Charlesworth, Weems and Maar.[19]

2.
The portrait photograph

In this 'imageravenous' life we lead, we might need to relearn how we really look at images and how we understand the different genres. A genre that is simultaneously consistent and ever-changing is the portrait and the self portrait. 'Selfie' was named word of the year in 2013 by Oxford Dictionaries, and social media, especially Instagram has facilitated the dissemination of filtered and altered selfies.

I first saw Anne Collier's slides series *Women with Cameras (Self Portrait)* at FRAC Normandie Rouen in 2018, consisting of eighty analogue portraits of women that Collier found in flea markets, second-hand stores and on the web. Many show the classic motif of a person with a camera in front of a mirror. Their uninhibited facial expressions show that unlike with digital photography, it was hard to control and adjust their expression when taking the picture, making these self portraits more real and made a good comment on our relationship with photography and women.[20] As Hilton Als writes in the accompanying text for the show, Collier's images:

> bristle with a kind of post-Freudian electricity; there's a pile up of 'meaning' that gets shown and eradicated at the same time in her pictures with their complicated underpinnings, including the idea of 'media', and women in the age of mechanical reproduction: Are her female subjects 'real' or have they been rendered 'unreal' by the camera, that which edits so much of the real world out to give us all those disquieting images of women with dewy skin, flying hair?[21]

For me, the word 'portrait' is synonymous with the Dutch photographer Rineke Dijkstra. Self-conscious teenagers posing on the beach; a mother cradling her new-born in the hospital with blood running down her legs; beaten-up bullfighters in the stadium after combat: these are all subjects for Dijkstra's large-format camera. She photographs people standing on the verge of a new phase of life, whose contradictory feelings about the transition are expressed in their faces. Her work echoes that of the great Dutch painters, and the Dijkstra-portrait, with its seductive vulnerability, has become an established term within photographic portraiture.

When I interviewed her in 2017, the year she won the Hasselblad Award, Dijkstra said that these portraits rely on trust: not only must she like her subjects, but equally importantly they must like her. To get a good portrait that

Anne Collier, *Women With Cameras (Self Portrait)*, 2017. Image courtesy of the artist; Anton Kern Gallery, New York; Galerie Neu, Berlin; Gladstone Gallery, Brussels; and The Modern Institute/ Toby Webster Ltd., Glasgow.

Rineke Dijkstra, *Kolobrzeg, Poland, July 26, 1992.* From the exhibition *Rineke Dijkstra, Hasselblad Award 2017,* October 11 2017–February 4 2018 at Hasselblad Foundation.

avoids cliché and captures their essence, they have to open up. It's about the dynamics between photographer and subject, and they create the work together. When people see her large camera, they realise that the process will take time – time that she needs to build trust and for them to become less self-conscious. Although compared with people in August Sander's time people today are more accustomed to seeing their own image, basically no one knows exactly how they will come across in the final picture; they cannot control everything in their face. Dijkstra's large-format camera, with negatives as large as a postcard, ensures that absolutely every detail comes out, making the photograph more realistic than reality.[22]

Nan Goldin

When I saw Nan Goldin's portrait *Jimmy Paulette and Taboo!,* from 1991 hanging on the wall at a school party I attended in the 1990s, I was more drawn to their story than to the people in the room. I was sure that these two knew something I didn't, and probably would never know. Famous for her highly subjective portraits of herself and her friends – her extended family – Goldin works in the opposite fashion to Dijkstra. She has shown us an ever-changing New York from the 1970s until today in snapshots that are often colourful, but depict dark fates, involving drugs, abuse and death.

Last November, Marian Goodman presented *Sirens,* a retrospective of Goldin's works, and her first solo exhibition in London since her show at the Whitechapel Gallery in 2002. New videos and portraits were shown on the first floor, and large-scale photographs of horizons on the second floor. The latter are less moving than her work on the first floor, which focus on her relationships with her friends. Her honesty is particularly touching in the film *Memory Lost,* a reflection on the darkness of a drug habit, where she says: 'Thank you for helping me out of the addiction.'

In a 2014 interview she told me that she photographs in order to record her life, and to stay alive – her work is her life.[23] Her advice to young artists is that they shouldn't do it unless they absolutely have to. In her opinion, it's art – it's not a job – it should be what you do to survive. Goldin grew up before there was an art market, where one was an artist in a more spiritual way. Today, her students only talk about what gallery they want to exhibit in and Goldin explains to them that art must come from deep inside themselves, and how they look at the world around them.

She believes that her work is best seen either in book form or as a slide show. Photography is the only art form that works in books in her opinion. She loves books, but originally wanted to make films and said that the slideshow is the closest she comes to filmmaking. Images should be experienced physically, not online she said. She is critical of what the internet, computers and social media have done to photography, since people lose the opportunity to truly experience photography when they only see it on screen. In this sense, she feels that she's lost her medium. She had recently attended a party for Magnum, where she stated that photography is over – it's dead, it's just a video game – and no one had talked to her for the rest of the evening.

We spoke over a late dinner during Landskrona Photo Festival, arranged by her friend, the Swedish photographer JH Engström, who disagreed that Goldin has lost her medium. He had just seen her spend two hours in the book tent, and said he didn't know anyone as passionate when it comes to photography as her. She had just launched *Eden and After*, her first book in eleven years, a result of photographs taken of her friends' children over a period of 35 years. The book also deals with the relationship between parents and children, as well as the issue of gender. In some images, Goldin portrays a child who wanted to be a boy between the ages of six and fourteen. Goldin has photographed children her whole life, saying that she photographs the wild ones, the ones who can't be tamed. She believes that children come from another planet – they know everything about everything when they're born, and then they forget it as they grow up. Or they're trained to forget it. She once overheard a friend's child, perhaps four or five years old, who asked a baby: 'Do you remember God? Because I've begun to forget him.'

Goldin's 2010 exhibition *Scopophilia* (love of looking, or as Goldin's friend Peter Hujar once explained to her, literally: 'fulfillment of your self by looking') was commissioned by the Louvre in Paris. For a period of eight months, she was allowed to wander around the museum every Tuesday with her camera. The exhibition featured details from various paintings she fell in love with, put together with pictures from her own archive. Goldin told me that she works constantly – obviously not on a computer – at home in her studio in Brooklyn, New York, with paper prints scattered all over the place, ready for editing. Her assistants are attempting to archive her work, a process that she described as a treasure hunt. There were many photographs that she didn't remember, and she's not convinced this job would ever be completed. She found it

Nan Goldin, *Jimmy Paulette and Taboo! In the Bathroom,* 1991.
Courtesy of the artist, Mariann Goodman and Galleri K.

comforting, however, that Weegee had big bags full of negatives in his garage when he died.

Goldin photographs what her eyes are drawn to, and told me that all her pictures are about memories. Whether they're pictures of people or buildings is irrelevant. 'I don't need to explain myself further', she concluded. 'It's all there in my photographs.'

Jakob Landvik and Ethan James Green

Both Goldin and Dijkstra are intrigued by the notion of the transition. This also seems to be the case with Jakob Landvik and Ethan James Green, who both work with questions around queerness. Landvik explained to me that he is captivated by different expressions of identity in a kind of search for his own mirror image.[24] The interview took place some weeks before his first solo exhibition *Without Mommy Interlude* at the SCHLOSS gallery in Oslo, 2018. He is a well-known figure in Norway, and was that month portrayed on the cover of the fashion magazine Costume as part of a focus on Generation Z. For the accompanying interview he said he works to promote the rights of his LGBTQ-sisters, and told me later that he identifies as 'queer' before anything else. To him, the queer community is his family, and his queerness is about belonging, a kind of inner platform that is rooted in who he is and what he stands for. Everything Landvik does revolves around this core, including his photography, with which he projects out into the world.

The pictures in the exhibition were snapshot-like photographs of his friends, several of them previously published on Instagram. *Jordan, Dagsen, Olof,* for example, depicts three young men looking dreamily into the camera on a summer day. The show was a curation of his archive, hand-picked in collaboration with artist Ida Ekblad, his gallerist, who also functions as a kind of mentor. The title *Without Mommy Interlude* was intended to describe a kind of debut, a metaphor for moving away from home, and entering a new phase.

Ethan James Green published his first monograph, *Young New York*, with Aperture last year and his black and white portraits have been compared to none other than Diane Arbus. The book contains a number of strong portraits of young New Yorkers, vulnerable and honest, including Green himself.

Jakob Landvik, *Jordan, Dagsen, Olof.* Courtesy Jakob Landvik og SCHLOSS, Oslo.

Ethan James Green, *Marcs,* 2015; from *Young New York*, Aperture, 2019.

During the first COVID-19 lockdown weeks, many publishers initiated online photography conversations, and the interview with Green by managing editor of Aperture, Brendan Embser in April this year was a highlight. It felt luxurious to sit in my kitchen, open my Mac and then be transported into Green's apartment in New York.[25] He talked about how he photographs his friends and acquaintances, mostly doing fashion work, and how he had just finished photographing first responders for Vogue. He explained how he shot everything outside, being extra careful, and revelled in the assignment, saying that it was an honour to do his first human-interest story.

The conversation touched upon the inspiration for *Young New York,* when Green worked for David Armstrong and got acquainted with his book *The Silver Cord* from 1997. Green drew from Armstrong's homoerotic landscape, and while looking at the pictures of the people photographed, he began mentally searching for the equivalents from his own generation. He started shooting images with his friend Hari Nef, the first openly transgender person to grace the cover of British Elle, and through Nef, met another subject for the series. He then met another through the next, and it turned into to a kind of relay. He shot his subjects wearing the fashion clothes they picked out together. As in the portrait of Marcs shown here, shot a few weeks after they got to know each other this portrait became the first in the series. They are still very close and often collaborates, with Marcs being a model but also doing set design.[26]

Embser points out that while there is a DNA of fashion in the portraits, it is even more about friendship. Green himself views his series as a record of a special moment for trans identity. Nef agrees, writing in the foreword of the book about how quietly revolutionary Green's work is, photographing this generation, preserving and recognising them.

Transition could also be a key word for Diane Arbus, to whom Green was compared. In the 1972 Aperture monograph on her work, she talks about how there are things that nobody would see unless she photographed them. 'Our whole guise is like giving a sign to the world to think of us in a certain way', she adds, 'but there's a point between what you want people to know about you and what you can't help people knowing about you.'[27] At the first exhibition of her pictures, the photographs were spat on. Susan Sontag wrote a critical text about them in the essay 'America, Seen through Photographs,

Darkly', writing that Arbus recklessly presents dwarves, transvestites and nudists as freaks, without empathy for her subjects. This is not how I read Arbus' images. She followed Eddie Carmell, for example, the subject of *Jewish Giant, taken at Home with His Parents in the Bronx,* NY, 1970, over several years. She loved to enter new worlds and go where she had never been before. When she was at a nudist camp to immortalise in vibrant images the people there, she was naked herself. She photographed to normalise her subjects, not to expose them. She wanted to depict the world as she saw it, and believed that the camera had magical power.[28] It is the same today with Green and Landvik, who are one with the people they portray. Their purpose seems broader than others from their generation, teaching us about a world we should know better, creating a new representation for the LGBTQ community and widening our understanding of gender and its fluidity.

3.
The sociological photograph

For the launch of Objektiv #19 with Temple Arles Books during the Rencontres d'Arles in 2019, we invited the audience to join us in making mind maps for the future. We also initiated a collective brainstorming session designed to identify what tendencies have dominated the medium since 2010. Throughout the past decade, the documentary image has been widely discussed. When the Dutch artist Erik Van der Wejde wrote 'photography as sociology' on his mindmap in Arles, it seemed an apt term to cover the new form of documentary work we are seeing today.

Independant scholar and photographer Christine Hansen and professor Sigrid Lien wrote about the documentary genre in our seventh issue, where they explored how photographers in this decade are capable of approaching both mundane and more acute political subject matter with their own individual accents.[29] I asked Hansen whether she saw a shift to sociology, and she answered that several of the projects she sees today span over a longer period of time and are research based, with an aim to observe sociological or societal phenomena. Asked about the political aspects of this kind of work, Hansen quotes the French philosopher Jacques Ranciere's broad definition of the political, a concept that he stretches to include much more than explicit political statements. The process of renegotiating what is visible in a society is a political activity, he states: 'Politics revolves around what is seen and what can be said about it, around who has the ability to see and the talent to speak, around the properties of spaces and the possibilities of time.'[30] An artwork or film can therefore reorganise the sensory hierarchies in a given society, Hansen explains. It can help shift the relationship between what can be seen and what can be said.

My very first essay on photography for the Norwegian newspaper Dagbladet was about the retrospective *Richard Avedon Photographs 1944-2004* at Louisiana Museum outside Copenhagen in 2007, and I realise now that this encounter could actually be seen as my first with 'photography as sociology', although this is not how we usually think of the American photographer's work. Avedon has said in several interviews that he used photography to examine himself as a human being, and that all the pictures he took were in one way or another a picture of himself. Calling his portraits investigations and open questions on which the viewer could reflect, he wanted to get as close as possible to his subjects, behind the surface, to pull out what they were trying to hide or forget, always searching for the truth in their faces.

Such portraits include those made in psychiatric hospitals (his sister was very ill) and at the death bed of his father, whom he photographed from 1967 to 1973. This work became the subject of his first monographic New York museum exhibition, *Jacob Israel Avedon, photographed by Richard Avedon* at MoMA in 1974. The recently re-published 1964 book *Nothing Personal,* a collaboration with his former classmate James Baldwin, presents the America they saw. The combination of Avedon's images and Baldwin's words remains an important document today, which is why the republishing of the book in 2017 was so welcome. It presents, for example, the family portrait of William Casby, at that time one of the last living Americans born into slavery. Here, he is sitting on a porch, surrounded by family members, all smiling, all evoking hope. As Baldwin writes: 'It is necessary, while in darkness, to know that there is a light somewhere.'

The 2007 retrospective painted a fuller picture of the photographer and his pioneering work, and what struck me was his generosity towards others and his commitment to collaboration, as with Baldwin. One can see this in the book *Avedon at Work* by photographer Laura Wilson, who assisted Avedon in Texas and documented his five-year long project *In the American West,* commissioned by the Amon Carter Museum of Fort Worth, Texas, to create a portrait of ordinary people of the American West. *Avedon at Work* shows his commitment and cooperation, warmth and generosity to his peers, and is a great backstage introduction to the project. Every photographer should be lucky enough to have another documenting their work.

A more recent example of sociological photography is Mohamed Bourouissa's exhibition *Free Trade* – a show that was awarded the Deutsche Börse Photography Foundation Prize in 2020 – presented in Arles on the second floor of a big Monoprix near the train station. The artist chose the venue, art critic Magali Jauffret writes in the festival overview, because a superstore provides an interesting context for his body of work, which questions the treatment of the unemployed and the humble members of our society, as well as the circulation of money and knowledge. This fall, Bourouissa exhibited photographs of plants in the show *Brutal Family Roots* at his Paris gallery Kamel Mennour, originally conceived for the 22nd Sydney Biennale. Drawn from his childhood memories, it reflects on how one becomes emotionally attached to plants, people, smells, movements and languages, and on how that foundation often becomes conflicted once we start to move around the

Φ MOHAMED BOUROUISSA

La Poste 2020

FRANCE 2,32 €

Phil@poste

Mohamed Bourouissa's work is on a new stamp in France, his *'Portrait d'un jeune homme noir, vêtu d'un «hoodie»'* (Portrait of a young black man dressed in a hoodie). 2020.

world: 'Plants, like humans, drop their seeds and sprout in new lands, or are removed, relocated and transported to be planted in places far from their ancestors.'[31] Both of his shows are fitting examples of photography as sociology, which could also be termed photography with a heart, photography with an investment, and invites us to rethink documentary photography.

For a long time, I have felt exhausted by the idea of 'documentary', and shows with this word in their titles have elicited a kind of numbness. The exhibition *Antiphotojournalism* at Foam, Amsterdam, in 2011 dealt with this numbness, aiming to challenge the role of the photojournalist in our visual world. Several of the exhibitors were professional press photographers, but had begun to question the genre. The curators behind the exhibition, Thomas Keenan and Carles Guerra, asked themselves how to tell stories of war and suffering visually so that people can really understand what is happening. They got the idea after Guerra visited the annual photojournalism festival in Perpignan, *Visa pour l'Image*, where everything he saw was so homogeneous, it felt the same year after year. They thought photojournalism needed a critical overhaul, not to cease, but to become more creative.[32]

The urge to reformulate the field led to the simple idea of putting together work that critiqued photojournalism, which was being challenged by several artists at the time. Guerra was very pleased with the discussions that the exhibition sparked, and told me that one of the most striking observations made is that the photograph can no longer be processed according to the classic distinction between the incident, the photograph of the incident and the distribution of the photograph. These three clearly separated moments have collapsed into a single click.

Take, for example, *The Day That Nobody Died* by Broomberg & Chanarin, a work that erases the distinction between art and reporting. In 2008 they went to Afghanistan with a large roll of photo paper and turned their car into a camera obscura. When something happened outside the car, they opened and closed the door to expose the paper in the car, documenting the events, but in a completely abstract fashion. When asked about this work, and how it differs from a press picture, the duo called it 'photojournalism for a public art'.[33]

They usually work with projects that investigate photography as a medium in itself, and their main questions are whether the photograph acts as a reliable witness, and whether it has a real political effect. They question the claim that we're so used to seeing images of war that we no longer respond when we see a picture of a dead body. Disturbing photographs can get a strong emotional reaction, they say, but the problem is whether or not the image makes us feel that we should act upon what we're seeing.

Jacob Holdt & Arthur Jafa

There is a book in my library, *American Pictures* by Jacob Holdt, that has followed me through every move I've made. Holdt became famous when he hiked around the USA in the 1970s with a small camera in his pocket. He spent the night where he could, documenting racism and inequality between black and white people. These photos became the slideshow *American Pictures,* published as a book in 1977. Holdt has inspired many who work with sociology within photography today, and is often compared to another Dane with the same first name, Jacob Riis, who a hundred years earlier, in 1890, documented the ghetto in New York in the book *How the Other Half Lives.* Holdt told me in an interview that he discovered the book by Riis in a store in San Francisco and stole it to look at it on the road. He also claimed that while Riis held the world's first analogue slideshow, he himself would be the one to give the last.[34]

Interviewed on the occasion of the exhibition *Faith, Hope and Love, Jacob Holdt's America* in 2009 at Louisiana Museum, still sporting his long, braided beard, and with no plans to retire, he spoke about his extensive travels with his slideshow to schools, trying to educate young adults about the hardships suffered by Black Americans. It took the museum 35 years to exhibit his work, but Holdt had always refused to show his pictures in museums, seeing them not as art but as a fulcrum for workshops on racism, and saying that is was only by accident that he photographed at all. It was his parents who gave him a camera in order to see more from his travels. He had never held one before, and taught himself all the technical aspects. He claims that although he wasn't a good photographer, he was an excellent vagabond. There's nothing wrong with the images though; he knows what he's doing when he frames them, as with the three black kids standing beneath a billboard commercial where two white children are juxtaposed with the text 'Independent Life', or the three black women in a beauty pageant smilingly giving the Black Power salute.

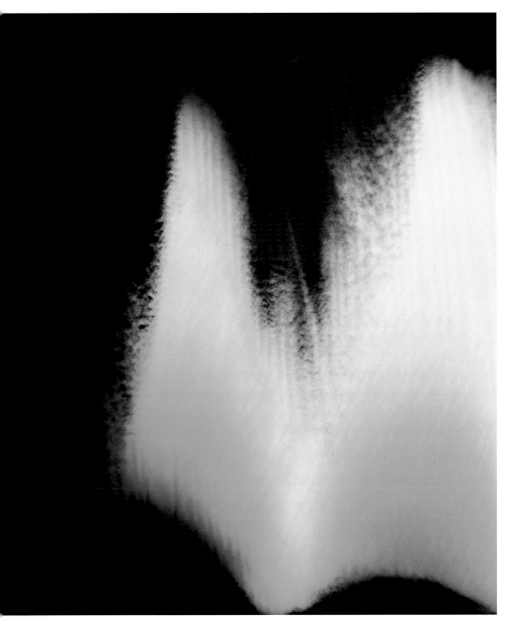

Broomberg & Chanarin, *The Day That Nobody Died* (detail), 2008.

Jacob Holdt, *American Pictures,* 1977.

Jacob Holdt, *American Pictures,* 1977.

I went with Holdt to the small Danish town Ringe, where the lucky recipients at a local high school sat mesmerised for several hours in front of his images of poor black people, very rich white people and poor white members of the Ku Klux Klan. As he told me in the car on our way, he just wants to understand racism, to see the bigger picture of where this hate comes from, and he wants to smother the racists with love and make the hate disappear. Maybe his thinking is propelled by the Scandinavian saying that trolls disappear when they're exposed to sunlight.

An artist inspired by Holdt is Arthur Jafa, who told me after winning the Golden Lion in the 2019 Venice Biennale that he wanted to include Holdt in his award-winning film *The White Album*.[35] In this film reflecting upon the issue of race, and in equal measure an essay, a poem and portraiture, Jafa examines violence against black people, juxtaposing private footage with news clips and disturbing statements.[36] It is just as hard to watch as his previous film *Love is the Message and the Message is Death,* and just as important and educational as Holdt's work.

In Jafa's opinion, this is a very interesting time, when we're experiencing many black artists on the contemporary art scene, and he's very conscious of how different that art scene was just ten years ago. When he and his colleagues grew up, society was essentially segregated, and the art scene was reserved for white men, with the exception of a few black artists, such as Jean-Michel Basquiat. *The White Album* was never intended as a political statement, but more as a proposal. Many people ask him what he wants the film to say, but for him it shouldn't have to say anything, just as a dance performance doesn't have to say something. It is driven by his need to study whiteness based on philosopher Cornel West's comment: 'What one cannot not know as a Black person in America'.[37]

The film has been screened and collected widely since Venice. I'm writing this passage in June 2020, and the police murder of George Flynn has ignited a long overdue movement for Black Lives Matter. The murder of Floyd is the latest in a series of similar horrific police murders, such as in March when policemen shot and killed Breonna Taylor in her home, while they were looking for someone else. Her murder did not trigger the same uprising, but her name and several others are included in the protests that are taking place now.

Arthur Jafa, *The White Album*, 2018. Still from Video.
Courtesy the artist and Gladstone Gallery, New York and Brussels.

It is true what Jafa said, about the change on the art scene and this is coinciding with many optimistic and affirming images from these protests that are published daily. For example, police officers taking a knee together with the protesters, or the young black boy giving the Black Power salute from the limousine rooftop – how much hope that image ignites! – or the woman with a face mask taking a knee in front of a row of heavily armed police officers during a protest in San José, California. This powerful moment was captured by photojournalist Dai Sugano during a march in support of George Floyd, and his image was quickly shared and praised. He declined my email-request for an interview, writing that while he was happy for the attention, but he didn't have time since he was currently working around the clock.[38] It is as if these images are driven by the pursuit of justice, and the photographers are risking a lot by being in the streets. They are not only defying the danger of infection, but also the risk of being arrested, as several already have been. These close-up images show photographers in the midst of the action, standing bravely in solidarity with the protesters.

Sugano's photograph was quickly compared to Marc Riboud's iconic image from 1967, where 17-year-old Jan Rose Kasmir offers up a chrysanthemum to the armed soldiers pointing their bayonets at her. The photo, taken during a protest march against the Vietnam War in Washington, was Riboud's last exposure that day, and he has described it as one of his very best photos, calling it a symbol of America's hope and youth.[39] Sugano's image is also reminiscent of the image of a man in front of tanks in Beijing in 1989 as he briefly stopped them on their way to the demonstrations in Tiananmen Square. The photographer behind the photo, Jeff Widener, said in an interview with CNN that he had been annoyed when the man stopped in the road. He was afraid that he would destroy the perfect composition he had envisioned. This irritation passed quickly when Widener realised how much stronger the photograph would be with the man in it. He became, according to Widener, a symbol of heroism.[40]

We don't have to go so far back in time to find a similar image, however. Four years ago, a picture from the protest march in Baton Rouge for Philando Castle and Alton Sterling was frequently shared. Single mother Ieshia Evans was photographed by Jonathan Bachman blocking the path of the police. Evans was named AfroAmerica Network Black Woman of the Year, and was also included as one of the BBC's 100 Women. She told the latter that the picture was bigger than her: 'I really did not feel iconic. I just did what I felt I had to.'[41]

Paul Mpagi Sepuya

Three weeks after the murder of George Flynn, artist Paul Mpagi Sepuya offered, through his LA gallery Vielmetter, an unlimited solidarity print to support organisations working to fight racism. The image takes a very direct approach, presenting a photo studio, with one of Sepuya's *Mirror Studies* in the background, and a camera on a tripod in the foreground, as if ready to take your picture – or for you to take a self portrait. It functions as an open question, a challenge for the viewer: what do you want to say, and how can you invoke the change needed?

In order to purchase the print, you have to email Sepuya with the documented confirmation of your donation. As he explained in an interview with Hyperallergic, he believes that non-Black curators, gallerists and museum directors who put up public-facing texts in exhibitions about representation, justice, inclusion, diversity, should make public their receipts for the donations. He also wants to see receipts from non-Black collectors to show that their interest in Black bodies isn't salacious and that they're using their money to defend Black lives.[42] As of September, the print had raised close to $220,000 for different organisations, and Sepuya has just reopened the fundraiser, focusing on voter suppression of Floridians with felony criminal records. Sepuya's request is for people to invest from $250 and up, to pay fines and fees so that over 700,000 fellow citizens can register to vote, with his print as a thank you gift.

This spring also brought a monograph by Sepuya co-published by Aperture and the Contemporary Art Museum St Louis on the occasion of his major solo exhibition there. As fellow American photographer Deana Lawson, Sepuya works to create a new iconography for black people, and also with a queer gaze. The book includes his early portraits, studio work with all props visible, some recent plates with collages, his mirror studies, and a series called *Darkroom.* This work, showing black and white bodies, with or without cameras, against a backdrop of black velvet, aims to challenge the nature of photographic portraiture. The title could also refer to the darkroom of analogue photography.

When asked to look back on his work, the word that comes to him is 'recursiveness': subjects, places and strategies repeating over time and across and within images. It began, he said in Objektiv #20, with photographing friends and himself. It has continued for him in surprising ways, the ongoing collaborations and inspiration to which these friendships have led, and in repeated re-photographing of materials in his studio space. Over the last ten years, he has been interested in deconstructing the making of images. The most resonant and impactful development has been the moving of subjectivity and identity (gendered, racialised, politicised) to the centre of how those images are made and seen.[43]

Frida Orupabo

My last example in this section is an actual sociologist, Frida Orupabo, whose collages are inspired by artists such as Kara Walker, but equally by people whom she follows on social media, and by her own experiences. Alongside her job at the Pro Center in Oslo, working to help improve sex workers' conditions, she has collected pictures and made collages since high school. She told me in an interview three weeks before the opening of her 2019 exhibition *Medicine for a Nightmare* at Kunstnernes Hus, that having a completely different background is a good way to access the art world. She applied to an art school once, but didn't get in, and thinks that's a good thing because a school might have shaped her in a completely different way.[44] Her career and popularity have recently shot up like a comet, and she is working on shows even though the world has gone into lockdown: a solo exhibition at Stevenson Gallery this fall and then another at Kunsthall Trondheim next year.

Orupabo finds all her material online, for her collages that question ethnicity, gender and identity. By compiling and manipulating them, she connects her personal story with a collective narrative. Her collages become a form of dialogue with herself, and this is her way of working around these issues. They have a raw, almost unfinished expression, but contain big questions about our common history. Orupabo forces us reflect on this history. She calls it research, a kind of study. She doesn't use a lot of text because to her the visual embraces more than text can say about the problem. She tries to make a connection between what has been and what we are seeing now, creating pictures around the non-white western body, and what it means. She says that she makes pictures of people, pictures that are about love and relationships, but they are nevertheless linked to society. A white artist

Opposite page: Paul Mpagi Sepuya, *Studio (0X5A4983),* 2020. Image courtesy of the artist. Document Gallery, Chicago, and Vielmetter Los Angeles.

who creates images with white bodies is never asked why they create images of white bodies, she points out. The white body is neutral, and is not automatically politicised by the spectator.

In 2017 Arthur Jafa contacted Orupabo after seeing her work through her Instagram account and invited her to exhibit with him in *A Series of Utterly Improbable, Yet Extraordinary Renditions* at the Serpentine Galleries in London, which was also on display at the Julia Stoschek Collection in Berlin the following year. Her Instagram account was included in the exhibition at Kunstnernes Hus, on nine small screens. The work has been purchased by the National Museum in Oslo and Moderna Museet in Stockholm. In a gallery, Orupabo said, the work is no longer in the semi-private sphere and loses some of its original feeling for her. At the same time, however, something else is added.

The collage shown here has a very special symbolism. The earliest use of the swastika is found in West Africa, Orupabo explains. Understandings of this symbol vary between different African, Asian and European cultures. It can stand for currency, resistance, knowledge, fertility and doing good. In Orpabo's work, the Swastika is a symbol of the relationship between Europe and Africa, and European colonisation, not just of places, areas and people, but also knowledge, symbols and culture. The first thing most people think of when they see the symbol is Hitler and World War II, and it feels right to take the swastika back to its original meaning. To draw a line back to what I wrote in the introduction, this encounter with Orupabo's work left me anything but numb.

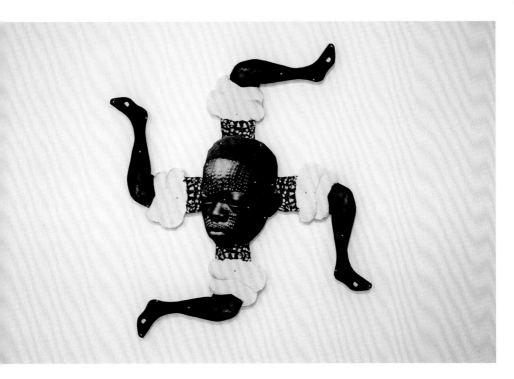

Frida Orupabo, *Untitled,* 2019, collage with paper pins mounted on aluminium.
Photo credit: Gerhard Kassner.

4.
The undesired photograph

I previously mentioned the image-saturated world in which we live, as has almost every essay on photography over the past years. Many books and articles have tried to analyse the effects of being so exposed to images, and there have been scores of exhibitions with titles such as *Image-Making in an Image-Saturated World* or seminars titled *Post-Photography* and even *After Post-Photography*. For all of us, not just those working with photography, this ocean of images is seemingly endless, and of all the photos that tumble around in our heads, there are some that we might not want to think about, that we try to forget.

The day the image of the toddler Aylan Kurdi lying face-down on a beach, having drowned in an attempt to cross from Turkey to Kos in an inflatable boat, emerged in newspapers all over the world, I wished I hadn't checked the news. It felt as if an ethical border had been over-stepped. Nilüfer Demir, a Turkish photojournalist, had captured the moment early in the morning on 2 September 2015, and it quickly went viral. According to the researchers behind the article 'Iconic Photographs and the Ebb and Flow of Empathic Response to Humanitarian Disasters', this image of the child, in his red t-shirt and blue shorts, had an 'iconic victim effect', instantly awakening our empathy.[45]

But did it? Or did the image push the limits of ethical photography? In mid-April, I called the Danish photo editor Thomas Borberg at the newspaper Politiken, to get his view on it. I had previously interviewed him in 2014, and on that occasion, he told me that each photograph he prints should always add something to the story.[46] It's about having confidence in the fact that the photograph expands and gives us more than the text has already given us he said. When I asked him how he felt about the image of the small boy, he said that we've seen violent pictures from the very beginnings of photography, that they've always been there. But, he added, since sharing is so easy these days, the total amount of images has increased, and the access to them is wider, maybe we're seeing more extreme pictures than we used to see. He continued saying that perhaps this image, of a child who looks similar to our own children, crossed a line for Western Europeans. He didn't want to print it at first. He always needs a very good reason to publish such a violent image, and the fact that other newspapers had bought it wasn't enough of an argument for him. Politiken only published it as the story grew.

One of the strongest images Borberg has seen, which is an image that still lingers in his mind, is of a couple buried together during the 2013 collapse of a garment factory on the outskirts of Dhaka, Bangladesh, taken by photographer Taslima Akhter. It was unusual for him to print it, because no-one knew who they were – Politiken rarely publishes a picture without establishing who is depicted. But this is still one of the strongest press photographs that Borberg has seen, and he points out how the devastating image created a debate about clothing production, bringing about something good, as opposed to the equally devastating picture of Aylan, which failed to lead to change. The day after that image was published, 70 people drowned off the coast of Libya and no one talked about it.

It has recently emerged that other unwanted photographs could for a long time be found on the website of the renowned photo agency Magnum. On 6 August, the online photography journal Fstoppers wrote that Magnum had been selling sexually explicit images of what appear to be children, potentially for more than 30 years.[47] In mid-August the agency took its entire archive offline. Olivia Arthur, president of Magnum Photos, issued a response on the Magnum website:

> Recently, we have also been alerted to historical material in our archive that is problematic in terms of imagery, captioning or keywording and we are taking this extremely seriously. We have begun a process of in-depth internal review – with outside guidance – to make sure that we fully understand the implications of the work in the archive, both in terms of imagery and context.[48]

Not happy with Arthur's answer, Benjamin Chesterton voiced a critical response. In his open letter of 20 August, he described the way in which Magnum-photographer David Alan Harvey had worked, writing: 'people actually think these pictures are "journalism". That it's OK to abuse kids if you get a photo story out of it. Magnum taught them that.' The letter ended with a plea to Arthur to suspend Harvey, which she did two hours later the same day. Arthur had not responded to Chesterton when I reached out to him in September, nor to my interview request.

More criticism of Magnum's approach was voiced in a long thread on Twitter by history professor at the University of Virginia, John Edwin Mason. He wrote that the Magnum photographers travelled pathways that British and French imperialism had created and which were increasingly maintained by the US: 'Imperialism & white supremacy gave them the "right" to go. Magnum's reputation came to rest on its images of suffering or exoticized Black & Brown people. People who didn't have the power to say no.'

Magnum's history suggests that it should be able to handle this crisis. The agency had just celebrated its 70 year anniversary when I wrote about its 2017 exhibition *Magnum Analog Recovery* at Le Bal in Paris, an exhibition with a focus on the photographers rather than the agency itself, and the ICP exhibition *Magnum Manifesto,* where the agency's past was the topic. Several of the people I spoke with said that Magnum could tackle any crisis, since it had redefined itself again and again over the years. The internal differences between the many photographers have been both a strength and a limitation, but are probably why the agency has survived for so long. Each crisis and dilemma has forced it to develop and rejuvenate, proving that it is still alive.[49]

Many see paparazzi images as unwanted photographs in our social-media dominated world, while others seem to crave them. Earlier this year, Prince Harry and his wife Meghan announced their withdrawal from royal duties. One of their objections was the requirement to deliver images for the Royal Rota.[50] The shock of learning how much they were expected to share with the British tabloid press led me to re-interview the self acclaimed godfather of paparazzi photography, Ron Galella. I had interviewed him in 2012 for his exhibition *Paparazzo Extraordinaire!* at Foam in Amsterdam, and here we discussed the term 'paparazzi', which comes from the name of the press photographer Paparazzo in Federico Fellini's film La Dolce Vita. Fellini got the idea of the name from Italian slang that describes the annoying noise of a mosquito, a contraction of *pappataci* (mosquitoes) and *ragazzi* (ruffians).[51]

Galella says that if he was one the of photographers who received the competing colleagues' photographs in this rota system, he would not be happy. On the question of what makes the celebrity pictures so interesting, to a mass audience he said it is all about the way in which we compare ourselves to others. We all want to be like them. Galella, nicknamed Gorilla, said that his mission was to get beautiful, natural pictures of the famous people he chased, and he told me that he had very few inhibitions regarding how far he would go.

He photographs one event each year, The MET gala, in New York. The press covers this event en masse, so Galella thinks celebrity photography has become exceedingly aggressive.
Celebrity photography today has changed due to digital cameras and phone photography. Coupled with the rapidity with which you can post an image and then see it on social media like Instagram or Facebook, this has created huge competitiveness, whether in the celebrity arena or on national/international news, between photographers and aggressiveness towards their subjects compared to Gallella's time he concludes.[52]

In the catalogue for the exhibition *Paparazzi! Photographers, stars and artists* at Centre Pompidou Metz in 2014, Quentin Bajac wrote about our fascination with this genre within the art scene in the essay 'Migrations and appropriations – Artists and the paparazzi aesthetic: 'At the dawn of a new century, when the Internet was redefining deeply the boundaries between the private and public spheres, a new generation, most of them born in the 1970s and 80s, set about appropriating this language while questioning this relationship, our relationship, with this type of image.'[53] Sociologist Nathalie Heinich explores this further in her catalogue text 'Paparazzi, Traders in Visibility', writing: 'Subject and author stand on opposing sides of the infinitely fluctuating border between public and private life, in an endless battle for image control.'[54]

One of the artists in the exhibition was Cindy Sherman, who in several of her series has questioned the artist's celebrity status. Since the 1990s, she has explored the construction of identity, and the nature of representation through her series of photographs in which she often appears in various guises.
Her acclaimed series *Untitled Film Stills,* for example, depicts the artist in different, stereotypical female film roles from the old Hollywood era. Her larger-than-life society portraits from 2008 have also been praised for dealing with ageing at a time when we are obsessed with youth. Sherman describes her process in an interview with The Guardian as intuitive, adding that her pictures contain hints of narratives so that people can make up their own stories around them.[55]

This September, Sherman opened a large retrospective at Fondation Louis Vuitton in Paris, and a solo show at her New York gallery Metro Pictures. In

Cindy Sherman, *Untitled #615,* 2019. Courtesy of the artist and Metro Pictures.

Cindy Sherman, *Untitled #614*, 2019. Courtesy of the artist and Metro Pictures.

New York, and via the gallery's online viewing room, she shows her latest body of work, where she has transformed herself into different androgynous characters. The figures pictured in the ten new photographs are dressed primarily in men's designer clothing and are posed in front of backgrounds composed from digitally manipulated photographs that Sherman has taken in Shanghai, Bavaria and Sissinghurst. The direct gaze of these figures, such as the man in *Untitled #614*, 2019, dressed in a cape and black pants with a blue flowery pattern, makes us feel as if we somehow know them.

In Paris, the comprehensive show is a career-spanning homage to Sherman, with works from 1975 until today. The walls are painted in different colours to compliment the work, which includes a new tapestry series where her self portraits are transformed into wall hangings. In a conversation with W magazine, Sherman says that she has been thinking about tapestry for some time, since: 'The weaving was not unlike the pixelation that happens in digital imagery.'[56]

The placement of Cindy Sherman in this section on the undesired photograph may seem completely wrong, her images being highly desirable, but the way in which she plays with representation, reality, fiction and celebrity culture makes a strong comment on our relationship with the images by which we are surrounded. Sherman has a large following on Instagram, where her gender-fluid, manipulated selfies reach an audience beyond the art world, helping us all think critically around the images we see.

5.
The exhibited photograph

This year has seen many new online initiatives and viewing rooms, often including discussions about the strange times through which we are living. During a talk in April between Guggenheim curator Nancy Spector and artist Asar Raza on Home Cooking – an online platform founded by Raza and artist Marianna Simnett – Spector warned that we're not likely to return to the same art scene that we left in March 2020. It's a harsh truth, but we may not be able to continue as we have done. And, after seeing pictures of the clear water in Venice's canals, we might perhaps consider whether the biennial should return there, and if we should continue with all the various art fairs that have been organised around the world.

Spector also touched upon the subject of exhibiting in the very special rooms of the Frank Lloyd Wright-designed Guggenheim. Amongst Objektiv's current missions is an on-going investigation into the ways in which camera-based art is exhibited in galleries and museums. One artist who has exhibited at the Guggenheim and who always makes interesting presentations is Wolfgang Tillmans. With a non-hierarchical approach to his imagery, he makes constellations of photographs, articles and notes, and he gives his photobooks, zines and posters equivalent weight to the gallery as spaces in which to exhibit. Another German photographer, Jochen Lempert, also excelled in this respect in his *Jardin d'hiver* (Winter Garden) at le Crédac in Paris this winter. His vitrine installations and wall displays gave each small image equal value, providing the perfect space to reflect on his black and white nature meditations. He is also a trained biologist, and this series continues work that began with *Sudden Spring* and *Predicted Autumn.*

I also thought about Tillmans' approach when I saw the first solo exhibition of Tommy Malekoff, *Night Suns/Desire Lines,* this January at the Los Angeles-based gallery Moràn Moràn. The two-channel video installation *Desire Lines* was complemented by a series of 20 small-scale silkscreen works, titled *Night Suns,* depicting nocturnal street lamps. The suspenseful music of *Desire Lines* drew me into the last room of the gallery, where the video installation featured clips from different parking lots in the US. The rapidly edited scenes depicted, among other things, a large cross being lifted by balloons, smoke and fireworks in different colours, a person in a Statue of Liberty costume, many horses, a man jumping on cans, a boy tap-dancing with cans on his shoes, a woman on a motor cycle with red smoke coming from its exhaust, boys in cowboy hats on horse back, a woman and a child pushing a shopping cart full

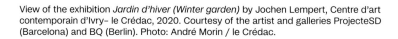

View of the exhibition *Jardin d'hiver (Winter garden)* by Jochen Lempert, Centre d'art contemporain d'Ivry– le Crédac, 2020. Courtesy of the artist and galleries ProjecteSD (Barcelona) and BQ (Berlin). Photo: André Morin / le Crédac.

Tommy Malekoff, *Night Suns / Desire Lines*, January 4 - 30, 2020, Morán Morán.

of groceries, all edited in a loop. According to the gallery's press release *Night Suns* can be considered: 'intimate, spiritual studies of these modern ruins … Giant bulbs dimly glow through nighttime backgrounds of pigment, high above the ground, reflecting onto the vacant lots below.'

At the same time in LA I saw the show *Souvenir* by Carter Seddon at Jenny's. Seddon took a more traditional approach to his instalment, his small black and white photographs hung in a straight line in the little gallery space. They are according to Seddon a record of something from his daily experience.[57] As he said of a previous work in the conversation with Lucas Blalock in *Objektiv #14*, when editing and organising single images, he thinks of them as comprising a kind of novel. His souvenirs at Jenny's made a very readable narrative.[58] Jeff Wall also once described his work to me as writing a novel, picture by picture. He believes in the ability of the single image to tell a story and starts every project not by photographing, but by trying to recreate situations and memories. Using the term 'empathic photographs' for the final digitally manipulated work, he insists that he is merely suggesting what has happened in the photograph, leaving it to the audience to guess what might have taken place before the image was made, and what might happen afterwards.[59]

I'm intrigued by this notion that something unexpected has just happened, a sense that is often conjured by Torbjørn Rødland. In the 2018 exhibition *Faithless Pictures* at the National Gallery in Oslo, for example, works by Rødland, as well as Louise Lawler and Fredrik Værslev were paired with those from the museum's permanent collection. One of the pictures from Rødland's series *In a Norwegian Landscape,* where he holds a plastic bag in his hand while contemplating nature, hung next to the painting *Nocturne* by Eilif Peterssen depicting a nude woman leaning on a tree by a lake. It created a sharp – for me, probably overly optimistic – narrative, transforming the repetitive nude female figure in art into the long-haired slacker male, and may in this way be the very definition of how faithless pictures can be.

Another way of playing with the unexpected is by placing a work in an unusual site within the institution, as did Éric Baudelaire, the winner of the 2019 prix Marcel Duchamp, in the award show at Centre Pompidou. His three-part exhibition consisted of a film titled *Un film dramatique* – a two-hour documentary made together with students from Dora Maar school in

Carter Seddon, *Tabby Cat,* 2019. Image courtesy the artist and Jenny's.

Eilif Peterssen, *Nocturne,* 1887. Installation photo by Nasjonalmuseet/Jaques Lathion.

Torbjørn Rødland, *In a Norwegian Landscape,* 1993. Installation photo by Nasjonalmuseet.

Saint-Denis – a flag made by one of the students, and finally a work placed in a small corridor, *Tu peux prendre ton temps* (You Can Take Your Time). As a preparation to the 114-minute long film you could see the 13-minute prélude, projected in a service corridor of the exhibition space. This work was something you happened upon, something unexpected. The project was commissioned through France's art programme, where 1 percent of the budget for the Dora Maar school goes to an art commission. This is only the second time the award has been given to a film rather than painting or sculpture, but Baudelaire points out how the school is situated across from a huge cinema production facility and said about the work: 'Rather than having an artwork in the building, the building and the life inside the building is inside of the artwork.'[60]

Elle Pérez

Of the many memorable exhibitions mentioned so far, a personal highlight was seeing Elle Pérez's 2018 exhibition *Diablo* at MoMA PS1, consisting of nine large-scale photographs and a collage board of images and written notes. I loved the return of the collage board, and as Pérez, who identifies as they, explained to me, the collage was an opportunity to do something less edited.[61] The nine photographs were there as works in themselves, and the board was a place for all the surrounding texts, thoughts and images to come together. Making this distinction was important for Pérez, who for the past few years had been trying to 'get it all in one image'. The artist had occasionally made a couple of these networks of images in grad school to provide context, but prior to this had never shown them or thought of them as individual works. They were images that Pérez didn't think could be viewed on their own but were important nonetheless.

The room was designed so that you saw the board last, after the nine large photographs. If you wanted to see it you had to go all the way into the room, and then it caught you as you walked out of the door. The artist hoped it might send you for a second loop around the room, once armed with this new contextual information. Peréz wanted people to see the texts – both the artist's own and those by other authors – after they'd seen the images, so that it gave context to the portraits, but wasn't a preparation for them. In this context, as opposed to that of a press release or catalogue essay, Perez said, the text had less pressure on it, working side by side with the images. I liked the idea of text without pressure, as well as images that need other images around them.

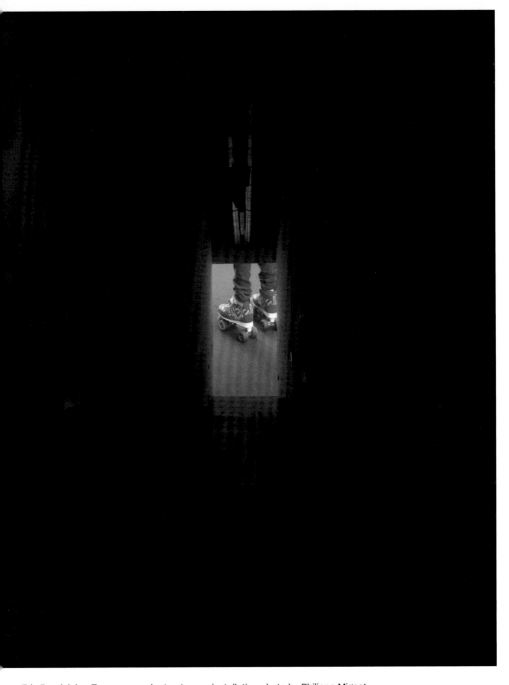

Eric Baudelaire, *Tu peux prendre ton temps,* installation photo by Philippe Migeat.

Elle Pérez, *Diablo*, 2018. Image courtesy of the artist and 47 Canal, New York.

In the year leading up to this show, Peréz had been trying to figure out how to construct a picture, taking apart everything they thought they knew about how photographs worked, and then trying to put it all back together. They had been thinking a lot about the notion of extended looking, how we see and how we look, and where these things linguistically and literally overlap. For those with marginalised bodies, there is constant visual evaluation. How you look completely affects how you are able to move through the world on so many different levels for Peréz, and historically bodies have been used as a measure for discrimination.

The portraits in *Diablo* made a great impact on me with regards to the question of who is representing who. They were taken with great respect, with the photographer at eye level with the sitter, whose presence is very much there, making this project a collaboration. This fall Peréz is presenting another collaborative project in the group show *Nine Lives* at The Renaissance

Elle Pérez, *Diablo* (detail), 2018. Image courtesy of the artist and 47 Canal, New York.

Society in Chicago, a show that is described as a collection of short stories or personal essays told from different points of view. It is part of a new platform called Feminist Art Coalition. Here Peréz exhibits three photographs, and has for the occasion made a booklet, *Lipstick Traces,* in collaboration with Maisie Mattia who has contributed excerpts of longer texts to accompany the photographs. Her text called *The Fifth Wound* (2020) for example, asks: 'Are you a man? No. Are you a woman? No. Are you a god in disguise? No. What are you? I am a blurry object.'

Laure Prouvost

Photography was not the main scope of French artist Laure Prouvost's 2018 exhibition *Ring, Sing and Drink for Trespassing* at Palais de Tokyo, but it was a very well-executed exhibition project with many elements. Still on my mind is a text painting, placed near the end of the show, with the message: 'Ideally here would be a door to lost hopes.' Who does not want to open that door? Prouvost's surreal, liquid and tentacular universe playfully addresses miscommunications, moves between fiction and reality, and challenges how we understand our history.

My hopes for Prouvost's 2019 Venice Biennale contribution were high, and I wasn't disappointed. I'm still thinking about a still image from a scene in her film *DEEP SEA BLUE SURROUNDING YOU* of a black man dancing in the hall of the pavilion, embraced by the sunlight from outside. The film depicts a beautiful road trip undertaken by a small group of different people, old and young and with different artistic skills, from a Banlieue outside of Paris, through Palais Idéal du Facteur Cheval and Marseille, before ending up in Venice. Palais Idéal is a place in France where the stone castle is built by an artist who plays outside the art market, Prouvost shares with me in an email interview this autumn. For her, the palace is an example on how to create purely from desire and shows the joy of creating. She continues saying that some people often calls the palace 'outsider art', but Prouvost thinks of it more like 'inside art', a drive, a desire from inside coming out.[62]

Even after several viewings, there's so much to discover in this film of many layers. There's lots of laughter and playfulness throughout, including a scene where we glimpse Prouvost's son with Agnès Varda dressed as a potato, but the subject matter is serious. In Marseille, the group climbs the rocks of the port, asking the sea what happens to all the paperless refugees. The scene

Laure Prouvost, a still from *DEEP SEA BLUE SURROUNDING YOU,* 2019.

with the smiling dancer in the pavilion taps into the deep-rooted conflict that France has with its colonial history and the day-to-day racism that people of colour experience.

To echo the experience of being an unwanted citizen, viewers had to make an effort to enter the pavilion. You had to fight your way through bushes before entering a rear door and walking up some fragile stairs. Once inside, you entered a world littered with debris from the sea, before walking through a curtain acting as ocean waves into the main room where the film was shown.

At the press preview in Venice, Prouvost explained that she had thought a lot about what France really is when she was given the assignment, as well as whether it is possible for just one artist to represent the divided country today. Having lived in France for several years, I was glad to see this conflict addressed. I remember interviewing Nigerian- American writer and photographer Teju Cole, who told me that Paris is a tough city for those with his skin colour. French people like to say they're not racists, but he still felt like a second-class citizen when there.[63]

Asked about the film a year after, Prouvost's answers are more peculiar, saying that it was her grandmother who taught her to look at the horizon and whisper secrets to the sand, and that these were tentic experiences. When she got the assignment for Venice, her grandmother had come to mind, the man dancing embraced in sunlight in the hall of the pavilion could have been one of the secrets that she told the sea as a child. Besides that Prouvost doesn't see France as a divided country, but points out how we need to know each other, feel each other, and how important it is to exchange backgrounds, tectures, smells and culture.

Prouvost has just revisited the film for her first show at LaM (Lille Métropole Musée d'art Moderne) in her hometown Lille, where she also engages in a dialogue with the museum's collection. Because, as she writes, there is another form of air in Lille she wanted to have some changes in the installation. The museum has a big collection of 'Art Brut' (outsider art), on which the topic of the film is based. Her fulcrum question is how can we feel what surrounds us? Like the octopus, which has its brain in its tentacles, she believes that it's possible to think by feeling. She also writes that there are no limitations between her projects, her works are organisms, they feel each other, they flow and grow into one another.

Given that our current travel restrictions will limit viewers to the inhabitants of Lille and the region, Prouvost is screening another film on her website, offering comfort in these trying times. The camera is focused on her torso and gesturing hands, which appear to be attempting to caress the camera, as she whispers: 'I will take care of you ... kiss you, I will caress you every day ... make sure you are in the best place ... next to the right people ... If you feel old, if you feel out of time, or not in fashion anymore ... I will be there for you.' It is a small pearl of a film to be watched wherever and whenever you want. And, as Nancy Spector said, maybe we won't return to the same art scene that we left, but one good outcome of the pandemic is that it has amplified the digital presence of art.

6.
The published photograph

According to publisher Marcus Schaden, the past decade has seen the publication of more photobooks than in the last 170 years.[64] Since 2010, we've also witnessed a self-publishing revolution, challenging the established publishing industry. After the excitement of this photobook boom, this might be the right time to rethink the format. For a weekend in September 2018, publisher Bruno Ceschel from Self Publish Be Happy and curator Ann-Christin Bertrand from C/O Berlin aimed to do just that with the seminar 'PhotoBook: RESET'. They proposed this 'reset' in order to inspire radical new thinking around the form and content of the photobook, which they felt was is in crisis, both economically and existentially. I was invited alongside Aperture's creative director Lesley Martin, editor Delphine Bedel and publisher Michael Mack among others to this three-day seminar. Bertrand asserted that the seminar was an important first step towards change.[65] Asked afterwards if the event met her expectations, she was optimistic, claiming that the most important thing was to have reflected on where the book industry stands, where it should go, and what future forms the photobook and its market could take. One participant pointed out that while books with pictures and text are conceived for a large audience, photographers usually make books for other photographers. Several others suggested that more diversity could be the future horizon.

Diversity might be a key word here. In the ocean of books, zines, pamphlets, how does one make something that stands out? When I wrote about the exhibition *Provoke – Between Protest and Performance, Photography in Japan 1960–1975* at Le Bal in 2016, it was with great admiration for the impact that the three issues of the experimental journal Provoke had on photography and on publishing itself. The curators, Diane Dufour and Matthew Witkovsky, together with Duncan Forbes and Walter Moser, wanted to highlight this important moment for Japanese photography.[66] Published during one of the most creative and turbulent periods in the country's history, it marked a sea change for photography. As the manifesto from the Provoke group goes:

> Today, when words have lost their material base – in other words, their reality – and seem suspended in mid-air, a photographer's eye can capture fragments of reality that cannot be expressed in language as it is. He can submit those images as a document to be considered alongside language and ideology. This is why, brash as it may seem, Provoke has the subtitle, 'provocative documents for thought'.[67]

Provoke was meant to be a platform for a new photographic expression, with the aim to update the visual language's aesthetic, and function as a provocation against Japanese society and its photographic culture.[68]

How can we make photobooks that can do for photography today what Provoke did in the previous century? I would suggest that they should function on the same level as novels, with strong narratives and clear intent. The first photobook that gave me this sense was *At Death* by Krass Clement, where the photographer followed his mother from her sick bed through her autopsy until after her funeral. There is a growing trend within photobooks today to combine the images with text. When Les Rencontres d'Arles expanded its photobook awards with the 'photo-texte' award in 2016, it marked a recognition and revival of this development. A year before, in 2015, Catherine Taylor and Nicholas Muellner had founded the Image Text MFA programme in Ithaca, with a focus on the intersection of writing and photography. For our 14th issue, which looked more closely at image and text, I interviewed Taylor and Muellner. When describing the melange of the two expressions, she used the analogy of plants: cross-pollination often produces plants that are more fertile than their parents. This is what she wished for the programme – increased fertility, a wildly productive site for future growth, maybe monstrous and beautiful, maybe nourishing, but always vital.[69]

Taylor also quoted an essay titled 'The Caption' by Nancy Newhall, which was published in the very first issue of Aperture in 1952, where Newhall wrote:

Perhaps the old literacy of words is dying and a new literacy of images is being born. Photograph-writing might become 'the form through which we shall speak to each other, in many succeeding phases of photography for a thousand years or more. The association of words and photographs has grown to a medium with immense influence on what we think, and, in the new photograph-writing, the most significant development so far is in the "caption"'.

Taylor argued that there has been a kind of continuing transformation – some might say reduction – of much writing into the function of the caption given the omniscience of the image. It might be interesting to think about whether we agree that language has become subsidiary to image in a caption-like way, or not. And, if it has, are there modes, uses or examples where language as caption might be re-imagined?

My personal hope is that producing more books combining the two expressions will make photographers experiment and bring forth such strong statements as Provoke was. The use of text might also bring more people in from outside the 'photography scene', making photobooks more accessible to everyone, and giving us the diversity asked for at the seminar in Berlin.

Duane Michals

The book *Duane Michals: Photographs, Sequences, Texts, 1958–84* was my first encounter with the use of text, and a revelation. It was inspiring to learn, when interviewing Michals in 2016, that he, at the age of 83, had made his first films.[70] These were made for his exhibition *Sequences & Talking Pictures* at DC Moore Gallery in New York, which showed a number of his short films or 'mini-movies' as Michals called them. The show also included posters for the films and several of his earlier picture sequences from the 1960s and 70s.

Duane Michals, *Double Talk,* 2015. Courtesy of the artist and DC Moore Gallery.

Duane Michals, *Paradise Regained,* 1968. Courtesy the artist and DC Moore Gallery.

A new illiteracy of images is being born, he said, and this is the result of the illiteracy of a culture with pretend language and pretend emotions. The images people are being presented with don't demand much. Donald Trump is the reduction ad absurdum of the one-liner-insult intellectual discourse. Trump is the ultimate destination of the trivialisation of language as meaning.

He said he didn't really pay too much attention to photography as a field, feeling peripheral to PHOTOGRAPHY. However, because he loves the field, he thinks he got annoyed by trends that he thinks demean it. The first trend is the Cindy Sherman-ing of photography as an art, and by that he meant the million-dollar-and-up prints. Now that it's become a product, students want to become photographers for the wrong reason. It's the 'hollywoodisation' of photography.

He's always enjoyed literature and poetry, in some ways more than photography because writing conjures up an imaginary universe that you share with the writer and create with them. Photography is defined by the facts it represents. It doesn't float in the air the way poetry does. De Chirico and Magritte are both poetic painters who play with facts, but contradict the facts with mystery in his opinion.

Years ago he saw a photograph of a young man on crutches. His leg was in a cast, he had no shirt on, and he was at home leaning in a doorway. Michals was very touched by his vulnerability, his potential future possibilities as a man, as well as his fragility. Although he's never specifically copied this image, it has crept into his work as part of how he perceives life. Maybe some of this is in his work *The Unfortunate Man,* whose caption goes: 'The unfortunate man could not touch the one he loved. It had been declared illegal by the law. Slowly his fingers became toes and his hands gradually became feet. He began to wear shoes on his hands to disguise his pain. It never occurred to him to break the law.'

Marius Eriksen
In the upcoming book *Arrorró, or A Farewell To Sioux City* by art student Marius Eriksen, there is something redolent of Michals in the lonely entertainer sporting a cowboy hat who juggles fire and just wants to be someone. Eriksen has self-published ten zines with text and images, calling them a kind of self portrait.[71] In this latest book, the fulcrum is old video recordings from

Marius Eriksen, *Arrorró, or A Farewell To Sioux City,* 2020.

his family's visit to the Canary Islands in the 1990s, juxtaposed with his own images from a 2018 trip. Eriksen explains that this project is about coming to terms with his own nostalgia, saying that memory is not an instrument for surveying the past, but an instrument for surveying the theatre of the past.

In 2018, Eriksen revisited the same scenes that were featured in his family footage, digging through layers of memories in order to get to some sort of revelation. He was hoping that his memories would actualise the present, as if the significance of the things long buried in the back of his mind could only be recognised much later. He wanted to look to his past to understand his present, calling his imagery a young child's memories seen through the lens of a young adult. There isn't much text in this book, as in his previous publications, but the few lines at the end enhance the reading: 'Approaching with wonder, trying to feel the things that I once knew. Then, later, I was caught in a strange dream, watching moments I cared for.'

Unable to give a thorough explanation of why working with text and images is important to him, he suggests that he finds great pleasure in combining both forms in order to give a voice to thoughts and feelings that cannot necessarily be expressed by one or the other alone. He doesn't feel he has to use text with pictures or vice versa to justify his work, he just feels unable to make one without the other.

Sara Skorgan Teigen
A fellow Norwegian, Sara Skorgan Teigen, published the book *Fractal State of Being* in 2014 and is now ready with her sequel. With the preliminary title *Sleeping State of Being*, it consists of drawings, photographs, 'hand-braided staircases' and for the first time, text. During a studio visit this summer, she showed me her latest dummy and explained that using text made her feel vulnerable and therefore more honest.

Her first book, made as a moleskine sketchbook, was an instant hit, the drawings and images seemingly pasted into the pages with dirty scotch tape, giving us something new and at the same time familiar. The pasted images amplify our longing to touch the photograph, to hold it in our hands. Both the photographs and the drawings have elements of nature in them, something that is important for the artist. On the cover and inside we see a naked person leaning over a puddle. This exploring character – the artist herself –

Opposite page: Sara Skorgan Teigen, *Sleeping State of Being,* upcoming with Journal.

29.01.18

10.01.18

reappears in her new book, where we see small cut-outs of her meditating, fighting against her scary dreams, and crawling around in the Scandinavian archipelago.

Teigen calls her books her studio, and it seems a fitting term: the book invites us in, and we are there with her, drawing and testing images together, involved in her process. In my 2014 interview with her, she called her drawings mind maps – physical manifestations of her thoughts, and meant to function as reflections on the world in which we live. This time, the handwritten texts in the books are recollections of her dreams, where she fights her inner demons, thus inviting a more complex reading.[72]

Carmen Winant

'Is it possible to leave everything behind? Is it possible to begin again, outside of and beyond every system of living that you've ever known, reinventing what it means (and looks like) to exist, as a body and its soul, on the land?'

These are the introductory words of Carmen Winant's essay in her book of photographs *Notes on Fundamental Joy, seeking the elimination of oppression through the social and political transformation of the patriarchy that otherwise threatens to bury us,* published by Printed Matter last year. She writes in her essay, which runs across the bottom of each page of photographs in the book, that finding this work, 'helped me understand what I was seeking out, a world where the rules and expectations of patriarchy did not exist, where violence (especially sexual violence) was eradicated, and where only photography could serve to describe both.'

For her project *My Birth,* Winant extensively researched the international lesbian-separatist community Lesbian Lands (or Womyn's Lands as they were also called – the 'y' replacing the 'a' to eliminate the word 'man'). The movement began in 1970s USA – only five short decades ago – when it was a white man's world. The gender inequalities in society and the lack of acceptance and protection for gay people made many women move out of the cities and form their own communities. These had clear rules: no men and no heterosexuals. The vast number of publications produced by Lesbian Lands – zines, pamphlets, magazines – show us how photography was an important tool for these women: making pictures became a way to reclaim and reinvent.

Opposite page: Carmen Winant, *Notes on Fundamental Joy,* 2019.

intellectual idealism, creative freedom, and fundamental joy. The *old way*—which for so

In 1979, Ruth Mountaingrove, Carol Newhouse and Tee Corinne initiated the Ovulars, a series of photographic workshops for women. (The word 'ovulars' is a replacement for the word 'seminars' whose etymological meaning is to 'spread seed' or semen.) Over the course of several summers in the late 1970s to the early 1980s, women met 'on six secluded, wooded Oregon acres' to take pictures, get inspired and share ideas. The Ovular's production was more or less forgotten until Winant, as she writes, fell into these pictures, finding them enormously seductive.

She often describes herself as a photographer who doesn't make her own pictures, and has always been attracted to photography that rejects photography, explaining that she moved into working in collage, installation and found images because she is distrustful of how seductive photography can be.[73] She started to use other people's pictures, often from books, because she wants to test the limits of photography. She loves the idea of bringing together different books from this very special period of time in the history of women's photography to create a larger tapestry of that moment, and also evoke the feeling of possibility and freedom. The project gave a wider audience the chance to (re-)discover these women, and to include their contributions in our photographic history, showing that there was (and still is) a whole world of women who made these photos and this world possible. Winant has likened finding these images to coming home.[74] Her text plays well with the images depicting women photographing, hugging, dancing, liberating themselves, and applauds this feeling of freedom. And since the images are from many different books – making it a book of books – it seems apt as a conclusion of this section.

7.
The fulcrum photograph

This notion of a book of books could also apply to this essay, since it is a text of texts, consisting of quotes from many different essays and interviews that I have conducted throughout the past decade. You could say that the interviews from which I've quoted here are my perpetual passages, words that are still on my mind. I like to interview other practitioners, curators and people working within the field to hear their thoughts about the medium. My intention is that it should form a dialogue through these many voices, instead of a fixed statement, offering a wider picture of photographic practices.

After looking through the twenty issues of Objektiv, I notice that the images that speak the loudest to me, and about which I've continued to think long after the issue went to print, all stem back to one singular photograph – a sort of fulcrum image. Asked about his work, the late Robert Frank said: 'When people look at my pictures, I want them to feel the way they do when they want to read a poem twice.'[75] The following images are, for me, the poems you want to read over and again, and it begins with a photograph by Tom Sandberg, taken in the nineties. When I first saw this image, printed on a postcard sent to me by a friend, it seemed to sum up my interest in photography, both as a practitioner and as a writer.

The black and white photograph depicts a man walking in the rain, taken through a window. He is blurry, the focus is on the raindrops. Before I knew anything about the photographer, the image simultaneously evoked both loneliness and authority, his oblivion to the rain, something that I later discovered says a lot about Sandberg. He was drawn to the darkness, and this darkness is in the photograph: the longing of being outside. Sandberg worked continuously throughout his life, investigating the world through his camera.

The moment he learned that he had incurable cancer in the late fall of 2013, he started working on what was to become his last exhibition, *Photographs*. The 16 black and white images were carefully selected. Some were reprints of works spanning his long career that have been exhibited all over the world; others were new. It was difficult not to attribute to them a special symbolism. This was especially true of the photograph printed a month before he died, of two airplanes that meet in the sky, forming a cross. The exhibition also included an early work from Sandberg's time at Trent Polytechnic in England. A diptych of a boy with a tennis racket, it is an artistic exercise. The boy is

Tom Sandberg, *Untitled,* 1997.

Dennis Stock, *Venice Beach Rock Festival,* 1968, from the book *American Cool.*

practising, and the young photographer Tom Sandberg is practising. Four days before his death, Sandberg made one last adjustment to a photograph of a plane in the clouds. He had a restless curiosity for understanding the world – a world that was black and white in his optics. As he said, some situations just had to be experienced through it.[76]

Dennis Stock
When I was looking through the archive, I re-encountered other favourites, and realised that these images were somehow linked to the Sandberg photograph. It's as if I'm looking for the same image, again and again. These new pictures all evoke similar feelings for me, and somehow they all more or less contain the same message.

For a book review in our ninth issue of *American Cool* by Dennis Stock – famous for his iconic pictures of James Dean at Times Square – we used the image *Venice Beach Rock Festival, 1968,* depicting a woman dancing on the stage in front of a festival crowd.[77] It is as if Stock has captured the essence of youth in one image. The photograph evokes the same feeling of nostalgia as that emanated by Sandberg's lonely man captured through the window. It is taken by Stock, but somehow directed by the young woman. According to Stock, she leapt on stage and started dancing in front of the crowd and the camera. Stock is taking the image, but it is the woman who owns the narrative.

Although Stock and Sandberg both operate in the black and white universe, Stock's pictures are more perfect documentations. He is a sort of 'Decisive Moment' photographer at heart. Stock himself says in an interview on National Public Radio that this image has a lot of Bresson's lyricism in it, because of the way the girl's hair flies around her and her pose.[78] She was like a contemporary ballerina, Stock continues, saying if there is a thread to be observed throughout his work, it is that he's relatively affirmative, not inclined to make fools of people, and loves beauty. To me, the image has the mystery, and also the authority of the man walking in the rain.

Astrid Kruse Jensen
Nostalgia is also the theme of Astrid Kruse Jensen's series *Disappearing into the Past* from 2010. All of her work has something of the same Scandinavian darkness that Sandberg presents, and thus in our special Nordic issue from 2013 her oversaturated portrait image from this series stands out. The woman's face is completely obscured by the strong sunlight. In its own way, this portrait also evokes the simultaneous mystery and assertiveness of Sandberg's man and Stock's woman.

Jensen explains in the text that accompanied the photographs that she began the project when she was pregnant with her second child, and was reconsidering the way she had created works for the past fourteen years.[79] She made a list of how she had worked before, including her need for control over colours and sharpness, and then wrote a list of what would be the complete opposite. She experimented with different approaches before arriving at using expired Polaroid film, where the unpredictability of the result was what interested her. Behind the choice of imperfection and lack of control, she realised an acknowledgement of personal vulnerability and a desire to let go. You could say that the sunshine is a photographic mistake, but for any Nordic person, after all the dark winter months, to be bathed in light can only be right.

Astrid Kruse Jensen, *Disappearing into the Past,* 2012.

Eline Mugaas
Saying goodbye to the traditional analogue film was also important in Eline
Mugaas' project *Go Gray Gracefully,* which we used in the same issue. There
is a pair of images put together as a diptych that caught my attention and
stayed on my mind. On one page, we see a female silhouette in Central
Park, and on the opposite page is the Empire State Building and a moon
descending.

Mugaas' project turned into a book some years later, functioning both as a
goodbye to analogue photography and a welcome to grey hair. The book – the
first in a series of five published by her own press named Dyslectic Times
as a comment to her relationship to text – is a photographic game, showing
her curiosity about the new narratives that appear when you place different
images together. She is interested in the mass production of a photograph,
and has worked a great deal with removing the layer that is the image, so we
are left with the illusion of the graphic in print. She calls it a 'weird darkroom
technique' that is all about the greyscale, and about the mistakes that happen
in the darkroom.[80]

Again, the diptych contains the mystery of Sandberg's man, the longing to see
the woman's face provoked by Jensen's image, and the nostalgia of Stock,
expressed in the lonely moon over a city that in many ways no longer exists.

Amalia Pica
The last image I find in Objektiv that is related to the Sandberg-image is
Amalia Pica's *Sorry for the metaphor #2,* from 2010. I first encountered this
image in the form of a fold-out poster in LACMA's booth at Paris Photo in
2012. The work is part of a series of A3 photocopies intended to be pasted
directly on the wall, available in different formats. Pica has also made several
billboard-sized versions, a format that can reach many people. A woman
holding a megaphone stands alone on a rock facing the woods and with her
back to the viewer.

When I interviewed Pica about her intention with this work, she explained
that it is a self portrait.[81] She felt she had to be in the picture, since this
was her utterance. She wanted to find a political voice, since she feels that
artists have a social responsibility to do more. It was also important for her
to overlap the political message with the romantic. To her, the photocopy

Amalia Pica, *Sorry for the metaphor #2,* 2010. Installation photo from Paris Photo, 2012.

Previous pages: Eline Mugaas, *Go Gray Gracefully,* 2013.

technique gives an impression of something homemade, making it romantic. This woman out in the woods is not as abstract as Sandberg's man in the rain, but both figures share the same lonely authority.

Throughout the issues, I found more works that in some way relate to Sandberg: the wilting flowers in Ingrid Eggen's work, a self-portrait by Arne Vinnem of him sleeping at Kunstnernes Hus, a collage with a woman in front of a landscape of mountains by Azar Alsharif, the mysterious pink fabric covering a hole in the ground by Lieko Shiga, or the trap car by Deana Lawson. All of these photographs represent longing or nostalgia, but one of the key factors in the images by Sandberg, Stock, Jensen, Mugaas and Pica is the authority of the subjects – something to be inspired by, and strive to have more of. Their strong presence makes me curious, these images become poems, perpetual photographs that I can pin on the wall and look at over and again.

Annotations

The inspirational photograph
[1] Objektiv #6.
[2] *Picture Perfect,* Objektiv #17.
[3] www.theguardian.com/artanddesign/2014/sep/18/sarah-charlesworth-stills-art-institute-chicago.
[4] *Kameraets Hus,* Ideer, Dagbladet, 23.02.2012.
[5] *Sarah Charlesworth by Betsy Sussler,* BOMB Magazine, 01.01.1990.
[6] *Considering the humanity of falling bodies in Sarah Charlesworth's Stills,* by Marc Guarino, The Guardian, 18.09.2014.
[7] Smithsonian Oral History interview with Judith Richards, 2012.
[8] Notes Charlesworth sent to Margo Leavin Gallery for 0+1 show in 2000.
[9] From the Estate of Studio Sarah Charlesworth.
[10] Found at the artist's website.
[11] *Artist Carrie Mae Weems: "COVID-19 Is Not an Equal Opportunity Virus",* by Alison S. Cohn, Harper's Bazaar, 17.08.2020.
[12] Email interview, 01.10.20.
[13] *Kunst som terapi,* Ideer, Dagbladet, 10.08.2011.
[14] From the catalogue *Dora Maar,* by Damarice Amao, Amanda Maddox, Karolina Ziebinska-Lewandowska, 2019.
[15] *Picture Perfect,* Objektiv #17, 2018.
[16] *Picture Perfect,* Objektiv #17, 2018.
[17] Email interview, 13.05. 2020.
[18] Frieze Magazine #208, 2020.
[19] Email interview 18.08.2020.

The portrait photograph
[20] *Kameraets kvinner,* Ideer, Dagbladet, 07.06.2018
[21] Anne Collier: *Women with Cameras (Anonymous), Anne in the Afternoon,* Text by Hilton Als, Karma, New York, 2017.
[22] *Rinekes perfekte portretter,* Ideer, Dagbladet, 09.03.2017.
[23] *Fotografiet er dødt,* Ideer, Dagbladet, 26.08.14.
[24] *Fotografiske forestillinger,* Ideer, Dagbladet, 27.03.18.
[25] The conversation from the 25th of April can still be seen via Aperture's Instagram.
[26] Email interview, 24.09.2020.
[27] Diane Arbus: *An Aperture Monograph,* 1972.
[28] *Vintage Arbus,* Ideer, Dagbladet, 13.09.2011.

The sociological photograph

[29] Email interview, 06.05.20.

[30] Jaques Rancière, *The Politics of Aesthetics: The Distribution of the Sensible,* Afterword by Slavoj Žižek. Trans. Gabriel Rockhill (London: Continuum, 2004).

[31] From the press release of the show.

[32] *Anti-fotojournalistikk,* Ideer, Dagbladet, 20.04.2011.

[33] *Forstyrrende fotografi,* Ideer, Dagbladet, 23.07.2013.

[34] *Tro, Holdt og Kjærlighet,* Ideer, Dagbladet, 31.10.09.

[35] *Rasisme og klimakrise,* Ideer, Dagbladet, 29.05.2019.

[36] From the website of La Biennale.

[37] *Universal Abandon? The Politics of Postmodernism* (1989), Anders Stephanson, Interview with Cornel West, Social Text, no. 21 found atindiachinainstitute.org

[38] *Derfor er bildet ikonisk,* online at Dagbladet, 08.06.2020.

[39] *Behind the Image: Protesting the Vietnam War with a Flower,* www.magnumphotos.com

[40] *The story behind the iconic 'Tank Man' photo,* by Kyle Almond, CNN.com

[41] *100 Women 2016: It is bigger than me, it is beyond me...,* by Anne Bressanin, BBC, 22.11.2016.

[42] *Paul Mpagi Sepuya Offers Photographs to Advocacy Organization Donors,* By Valentina Di Liscia, Hyperallergic, 02.06.2020.

[43] *Capturing a Decade,* Objektiv #20.

[44] *Jeg finner alt mitt materiale på nett,* Ideer, Dagbladet, 12.02.2019.

The undesired photograph

[45] Paul Slovic, Daniel Västfjäll, Arvid Erlandsson and Robin Gregory, *Iconic photographs and the ebb and flow 45 of empathic response to humanitarian disasters,* PNAS, 24 January 2017, first published 10 January 2017.

[46] *Visuell ukultur,* Ideer, Dagbladet, 06.05.2014.

[47] *Magnum Photos Is Selling Images of Alleged Child Sexual Abuse on Its Website,* by Andy Day, FStoppers, 06.08.2020.

[48] *A Statement From Our President Regarding the Magnum Archive Internal Review,* by Olivia Arthur, found at Magnum's website.

[49] *Magnums fotografiske magi,* Ideer, Dagbladet, 19.04.2017.

[50] The Royal Rota was established more than 40 years ago as a way of giving UK print and broadcast media exclusive inside access to the official engagements of members of the Royal Family.

[51] *Paparazzigudfaren,* Ideer, Dagbladet, 12.07.2012.

[52] Email interview, 05.04.2020.
[53] From the catalogue of the show *Paparazzi! Photographers, stars and artists,* published by Centre Pompidou-Metz and Flammarion, 2014.
[54] Ibid.
[55] Cindy Sherman: *'Why am I in these photos?',* Interview by Tim Adams, 03.07.2016.
[56] *Cindy Sherman's Enigmatic Self-Portraits Take Over the Louis Vuitton Foundation,* by Kat Herriman, W Magazine, 23.09.2020.

The exhibited photograph
[57] Email interview 06.10.2020.
[58] *Normal Pictures, The Flexible Image,* Objektiv #14, 2016.
[59] *Filmatiske fotografier,* Ideer, Dagbladet, 17.03.2015.
[60] Email interview, 02.07.2020.
[61] *Picture Perfect,* Objektiv #18, 2018
[62] Email interview, 09.10.2020.
[63] *En førsteklasses borger,* Ideer, Dagbladet, 30.08.2018.

The published photograph
[64] *Kunsten å få fotografi ut til fotfolket,* Ideer, Dagbladet, 15.09.15.
[65] *Nature,* British Journal of Photography, Issue #7878, 2018.
[66] The exhibition was conceived and produced by LE BAL with Albertina (Vienna), Fotomuseum Winterthur (Switzerland) and Art Institute of Chicago.
[67] *Provoke, Provocative Materials for Thought,* First issue, 1 November 1968.
[68] *Japansk fotokunst provoserte i sin samtid. Hvem provoserer i dag?,* Ideer, Dagbladet, 29.09.16.
[69] *Making Bridges, The Flexible Image,* Objektiv #14, 2016.
[70] *Jeg har sett fremtida og den er «fuck»,* Ideer, Dagbladet, 09.06.2016.
[71] Email interview, 27.07.2020.
[72] *Når fotobøker blir viktige utstillingsrom,* Ideer, Dagbladet, 30.10.2014.
[73] Carmen Winant, Objektiv #20, 2019.
[74] *Lesbian Lands, Carmen Winant and the Ovulars,* Camera Austria 149, 2020.

The fulcrum photograph
[75] Frank wrote the quote in 1951 and it was published in *Life* Announces the Winners of the Young Photographers' Contest, *Life* vol. 31 (November 26, 1951). It was also quoted in Robert Frank: *Moving Out,* (National Gallery of Art and Scalo, 1994).

[76] *Sandbergs testamente,* Dagbladet, 20.02.2014.
[77] Book review by Jorunn Rike and Terje Thorsen from the bookstore Tronsmo in Oslo.
[78] *The Picture Show, Photography Master Dennis Stock Dies,* by Claire O'Neill, online at NPR,13.01. 2010.
[79] *Nordic Now!,* special issue of Objektiv, 2013.
[80] *Fotobøker er det nye visningsrom,* Ideer, Dagbladet, 05.07.2017.
[81] Objektiv #8, 2013.

Editor-in-chief
Nina Strand

Editor
Melissa Larner

Editorial board
Lucas Blalock, Ida Kierulf, Brian Sholis, Susanne Østby Sæther

Design
Madoka Rindal

Repro and print
Narayana Press, Denmark

ISSN: 1891-6198

Objektiv is funded by
Arts Council Norway, Fritt Ord and Norwegian Photographic Fund

All images courtesy of the artists/BONO.

After ten years of exploring the magazine format, Objektiv wishes to go more in-depth with its content. Twice a year, we'll produce an essay-publication, a long text written by a single author accompanied by photographs. This change for Objektiv comes from a wish to widen our understanding of photography and to make something that will last longer than the ephemeral life of the magazine. This text contains quotes from previous texts, reviews and interviews conducted by the author, all of which were read and approved by the subjects at the time.

Published by Objektiv Forlag AS

Supported by
Arts Council Norway

FRITT ORD

NORSK
FOTOGRAFISK
FOND